THE GOLF SWING

SIX STEPS TO YOUR BEST SWING

Stephen Aumock

THE GOLF SWING

SIX STEPS TO YOUR BEST SWING

Stephen Aumock

Circumference Press

The Golf Swing: Six Steps to Your Best Swing

Copyright © 2015 by Stephen Aumock
Published by Circumference Press

All rights reserved. This book may not be used or reproduced in any manner, in whole or in part, stored in a retrieval system or transmitted in any form (by electronic, mechanical, photocopied, recorded or other means) without written permission from the author, except as permitted by United States copyright law.

No liability is assumed with respect to the use of information contained herein. While every precaution has been taken in the preparation of this book, the author assumes no responsibility for errors or omissions. Neither is any liability assumed for damages resulting from the use of information contained herein.

Cover art by Jill Christianson
Layout by Jonathan Peters, PhD

ISBN: 978-0-9903262-2-9

Printed in the United States of America

Acknowledgments

To my mother and father for their unwavering love and encouragement.
To my brothers, Michael and A.J., for their support and guidance.
To Ian Harris for giving more to me that I could ever repay.
To Mike Bylen for your friendship and mentorship through the years.
To Marten Olander for showing me the world.
To the gentlemen of the PHL.
To Hank Haney for showing me how to do things right.
To Rich Allen for being a great coach.

And to my students who have made my life so rewarding.

Table of Contents

FOREWORD	1
INTRODUCTION	5
STEP 1: ADDRESSING THE BALL, "THE FOUNDATION"	9
STEP 2: THE TAKE-AWAY, "THE DYNAMIC SET-UP"	39
STEP 3: TOP OF THE SWING, "THE EXCHANGE"	49
STEP 4: PRE-IMPACT, "THE GATHERING STORM"	63
STEP 5: POST IMPACT, "FULLY EXTENDED"	71
STEP 6: FOLLOW THROUGH, "CATCHING THE SPEED"	87
CONCLUSION	99

FOREWORD

In the spring of 1992, I met Stephen Aumock. It was obvious to me that he was highly motivated and a keen student of the game.

He had driven from Tuscaloosa, Alabama to McKinney, Texas for a single golf lesson with me. That's 24 hours of driving for a 45 minute golf lesson. He arrived at 8:00 AM and began hitting balls to get ready for the lesson... set for 2:00 PM! Before we started, I asked, "Are you tired yet, bud?"

I quickly learned how passionate he is about improving and being the best he can be.

After he graduated from University of Alabama, I asked Stephen to teach for me. He didn't hesitate to accept my offer. Stephen worked his way up the ranks from Teaching Assistant, to Head Instructor, to Director of Instruction. We ultimately became business partners and we still own a golf course in Texarkana, Texas.

I don't know if there is anyone who has studied golf instruction more or brought more passion to their teaching than Stephen. He has a "leave no stone unturned" attitude in his teaching, and it shows in his students' success. He has helped golfers around the world and on every tour.

I know the knowledge he shares in the book will help take your swing to the next level. The easy-to-apply principles laid out here can be used as a "true north" on your full swing compass. It is a great read as well as a reference guide that you will want to revisit regularly.

Work hard on your swing, follow the plan Stephen has laid out for you, and keep a great attitude. I know that you will achieve your goals.

Good Golfing,

Hank Haney
1993 PGA Teach of the Year

INTRODUCTION

For more than 35 years, I have been fascinated with the golf swing. Specifically, I have been fascinated by how the best ball-strikers swing the club.

It started in Rochester, Michigan when I was a caddie at Great Oaks Country Club. I would study the swings of the best players at the club to see what made them play so well. I would ask them what they were working on or feeling in their swing. It was a great education for a young man aspiring to a career in golf.

As a kid, I received an old VHS tape of *Shell's Wonderful World of Golf, Hogan vs. Snead*. I bet I watched that match over 100 times during those cold Michigan winters. Each golfer had such effective motions. I loved dissecting what they did, especially Ben Hogan. In that match, Mr. Hogan hit every green in regulation. The command he had of his ball inspired me to dig even deeper into the unique motion that is the golf swing. I have studied and worked with many tour professionals over the years, but to this day, I consider the swings of Hogan and Snead to be the finest.

During my time in this great game, I have taught over 20,000 golf lessons in 13 different countries to everyone from first-time golfers to PGA Tour winners. My students have ranged in age from 3 to 93! I have come to believe that it is helpful to have a clear concept of what one is trying to achieve in their own swing.

It has been my professional mission to distill the golf swing down into simple steps that allow anyone to strike the ball better than they ever have in a powerful and consistent way.

I've refined this model swing over my years by looking at endless hours of video, thinking through the swing during most of my waking (and many of my sleeping) hours, and discussing the swing to exhaustion with some of the greatest teaching and playing minds in the game.

I am eager to share the fruits of my labor with you in the following pages. I know that if you are patient with yourself and work hard on the items I have laid out for you, there is no limit to your improvement. My hope is that you will use this book as a formula and a reference for building improvements into your swing.

The steps described in this book are not the latest instruction "fad"; they are time-tested checkpoints that produce a simple and efficient golf swing. Being aware of these checkpoints allows you to instantly increase your confidence because you will have a specific direction for your swing improvement, from start to finish.

This is not to say that all golf swings should look alike. There will be variations between any two golf swings based on physical structure, flexibility, temperament, athleticism, etc. Those variations, much like a fingerprint, are what will make each swing unique. While this books describes what I feel is the most efficient way to swing the golf club, one must be sensitive to their own personal tendencies.

The great ball strikers from every generation have a self-created formula that allows them to play superior golf; you must do the same. As you work on your swing, take careful note of what those swings that get results feel like. Do your best to blend those feelings into your custom swing. Two golfers may be in a similar position, but they will have completely different feelings about their swing.

Let's be clear, there are only two true "positions" in the golf swing: set-up and finish. The four other positions I describe in this book are what I call "pass-through" positions. They are highly effective when used as static references, but are ultimately meant to be fluid aspects of the full swing.

Developing the **6 Step Swing** takes dedicated practice. There is no substitute for beating balls, making practice swings at home, and "shadow boxing" by moving through the **6 Step Swing** in a mirror without a club. Training your body to move through the specific motor patterns described in these pages takes effort. It is easy to be distracted by the latest golf publication or instructional video. It takes focus to stay the course and burn the **6 Step Swing** into your muscle memory. I know you will be glad you did when you are able to tap into your true potential as a golfer and start hitting your purest shots consistently.

With practice, you can build a deeper understanding of your swing that will allow you to design the accurate framework of your own personal cause and effect. You'll understand why your shots miss to the right and left, why you hit fat or thin shots. Practice helps alleviate the frustration of not knowing what is causing your misses. You'll be able to fix your shots "on the fly" while you are playing.

We all get off track occasionally on the golf course, but when you understand your swing, you can hold your round together and often hit your best shots on the back nine. This will give you confidence heading into the next round. Understanding and grooving the **6 Step Swing** makes all this possible.

> *"Golf is a game in which you can exhaust yourself but never your subject."*
> —Arnold Palmer

ADDRESSING THE BALL
"The Foundation"

THE GRIP

Your only contact with the club is through your hands, so it is important to place them on the club in a way that gives you a feeling of power and control. Your hands need to be placed on the club such that your wrists can hinge properly and the club can travel on the proper path throughout the swing.

To understand the proper grip, allow me to break it down by hand…

> *"Good golf begins with a good grip"*
> —Ben Hogan,
>   *The Modern Fundamentals of Golf*

THE LEFT HAND

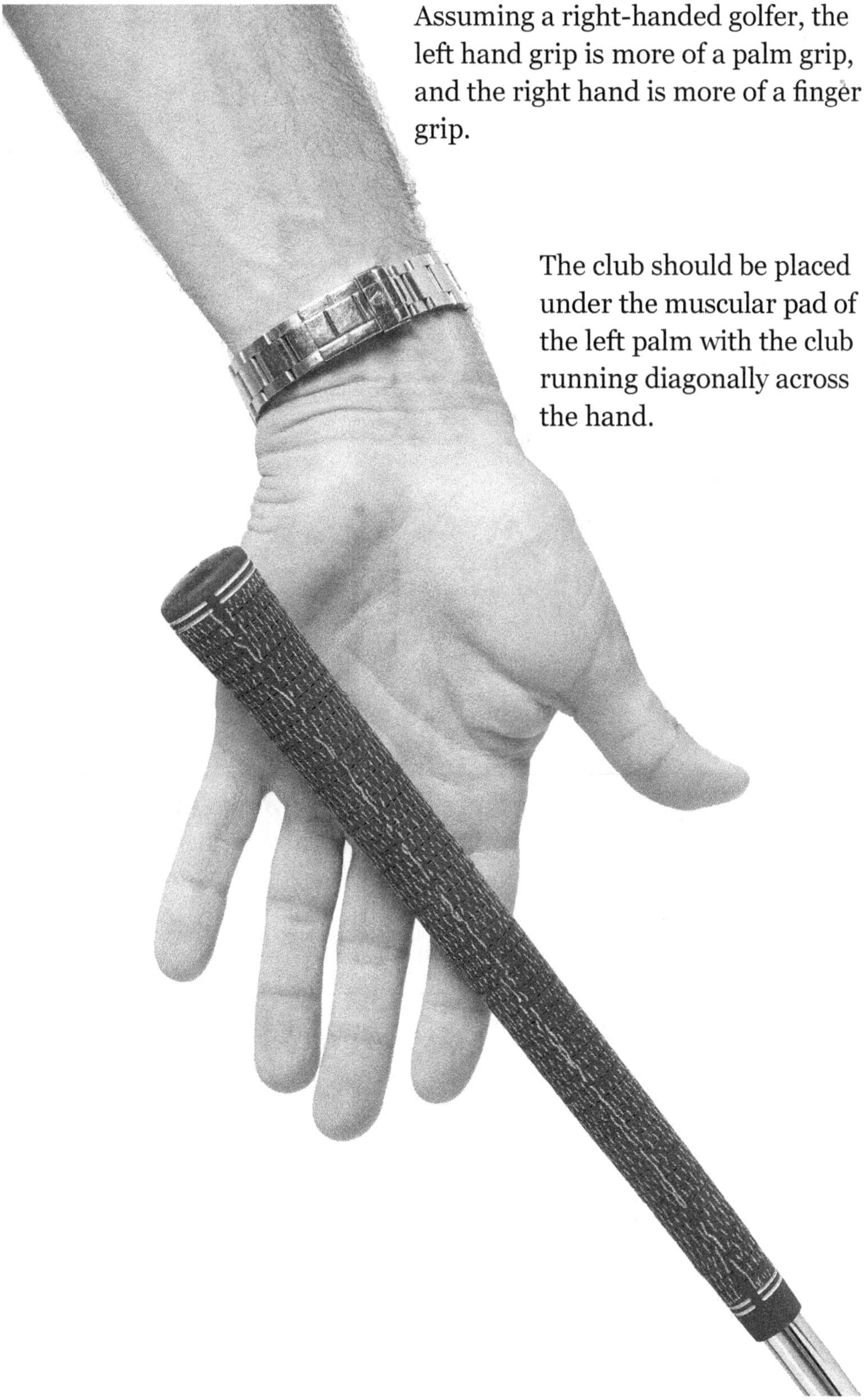

Assuming a right-handed golfer, the left hand grip is more of a palm grip, and the right hand is more of a finger grip.

The club should be placed under the muscular pad of the left palm with the club running diagonally across the hand.

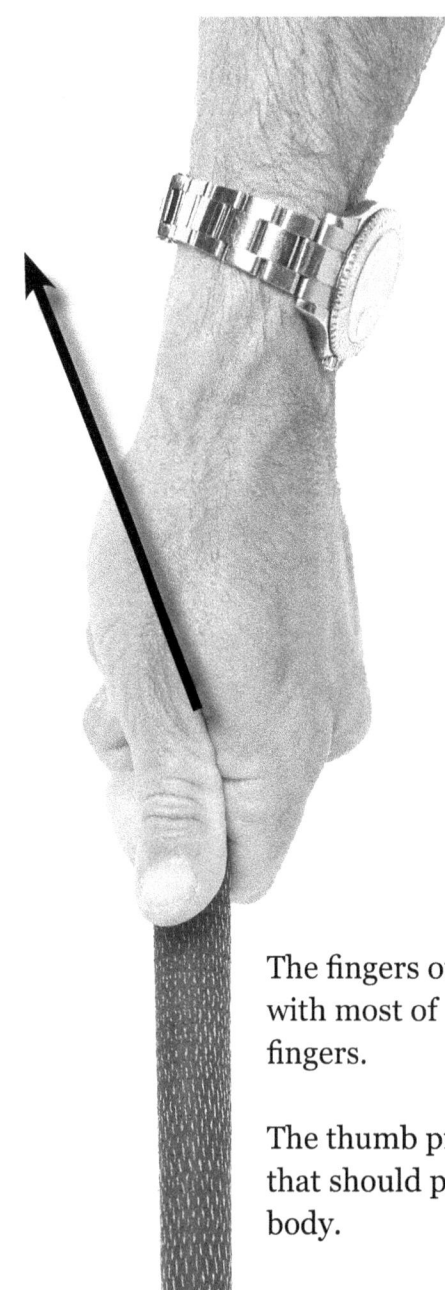

The fingers of the left hand wrap around the club with most of the grip pressure in the last three fingers.

The thumb pinches into the hand, creating a line that should point at the right side of the player's body.

Step 1

PINCHING THE THUMBS

Notice how the thumbs are tight against the sides of the hand, creating a seam.

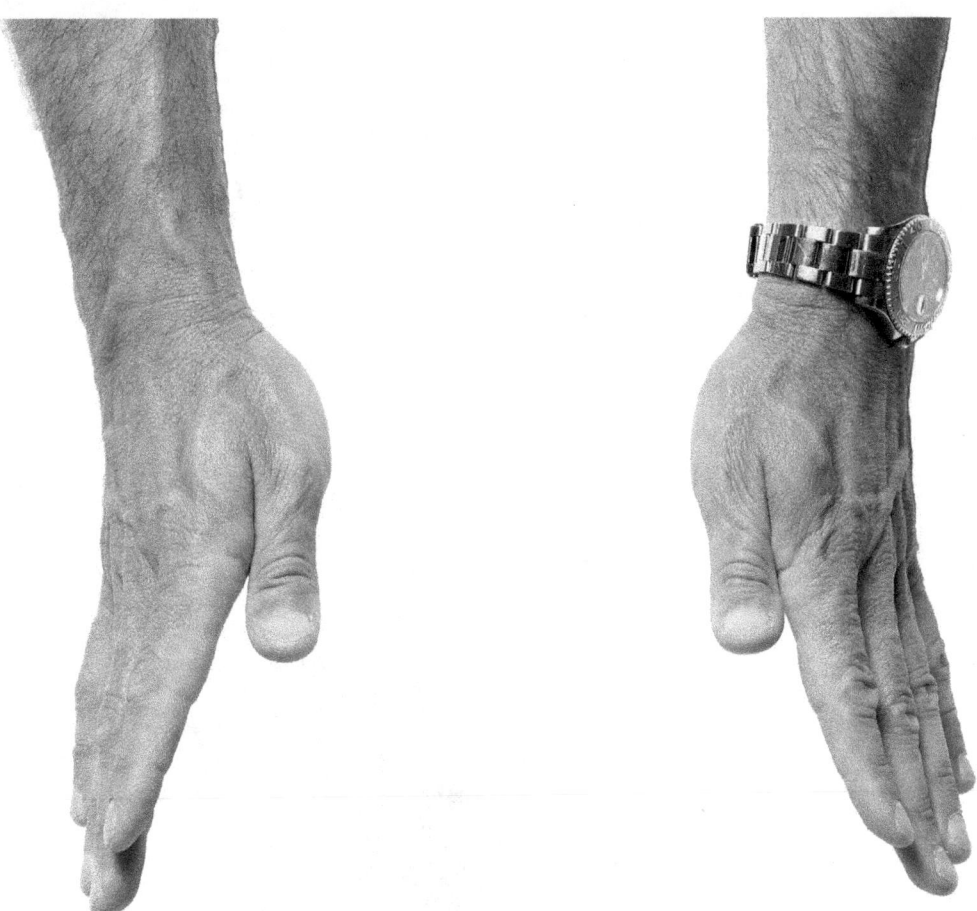

By pinching the thumb and index finger together, the golfer has greater control of the club, and can deliver the club face squarely to the ball with consistently.

THE RIGHT HAND GRIP IS A BIT MORE INTRICATE.

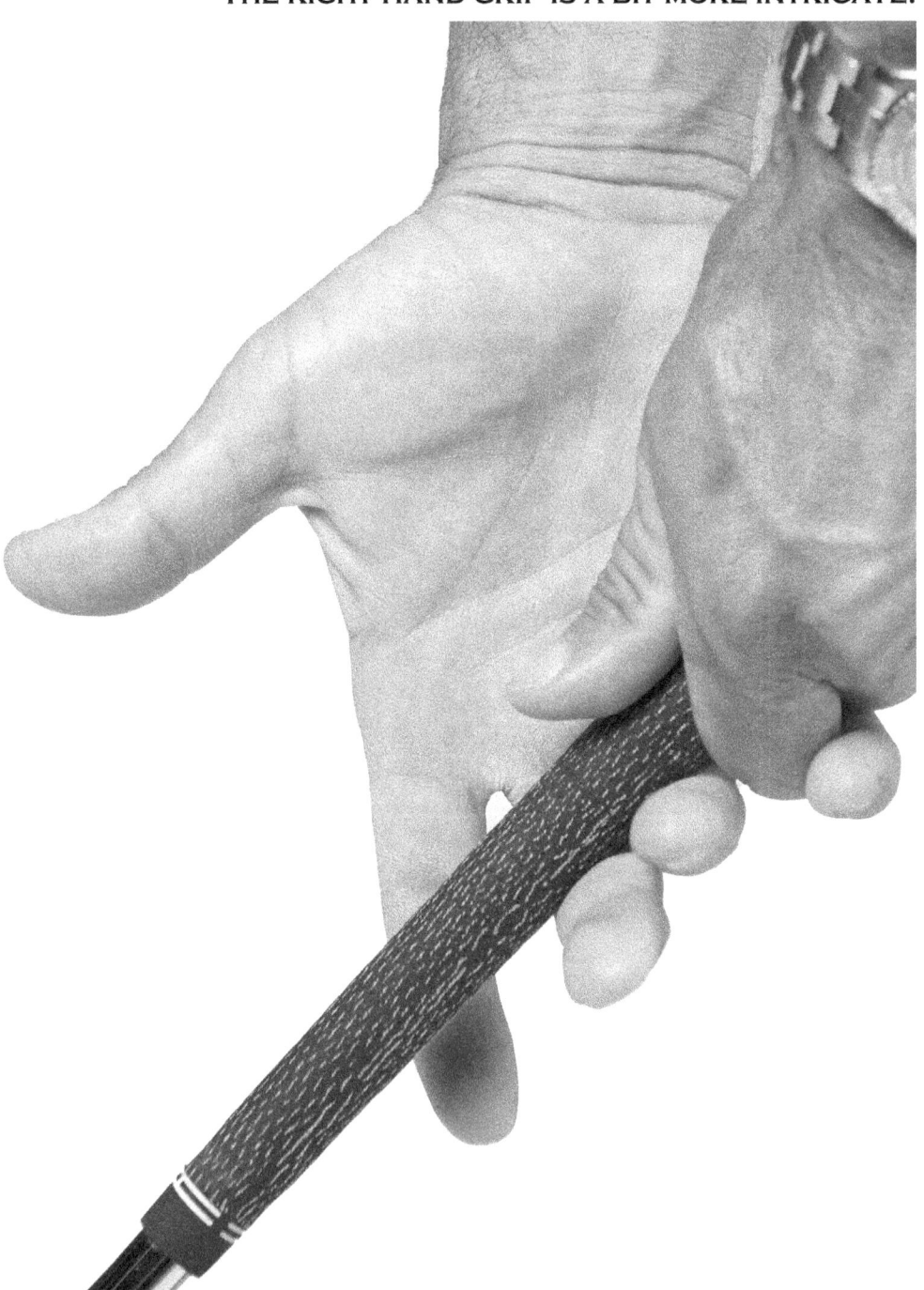

Many golfers tend to put the club too far into the palm of the right hand. By doing so, the golfer takes some of the "powerful lash" out of their golf swing. The right hand will not hinge correctly, which will not enable the golfer to put as much pressure as possible into the back of the ball.

Step 1

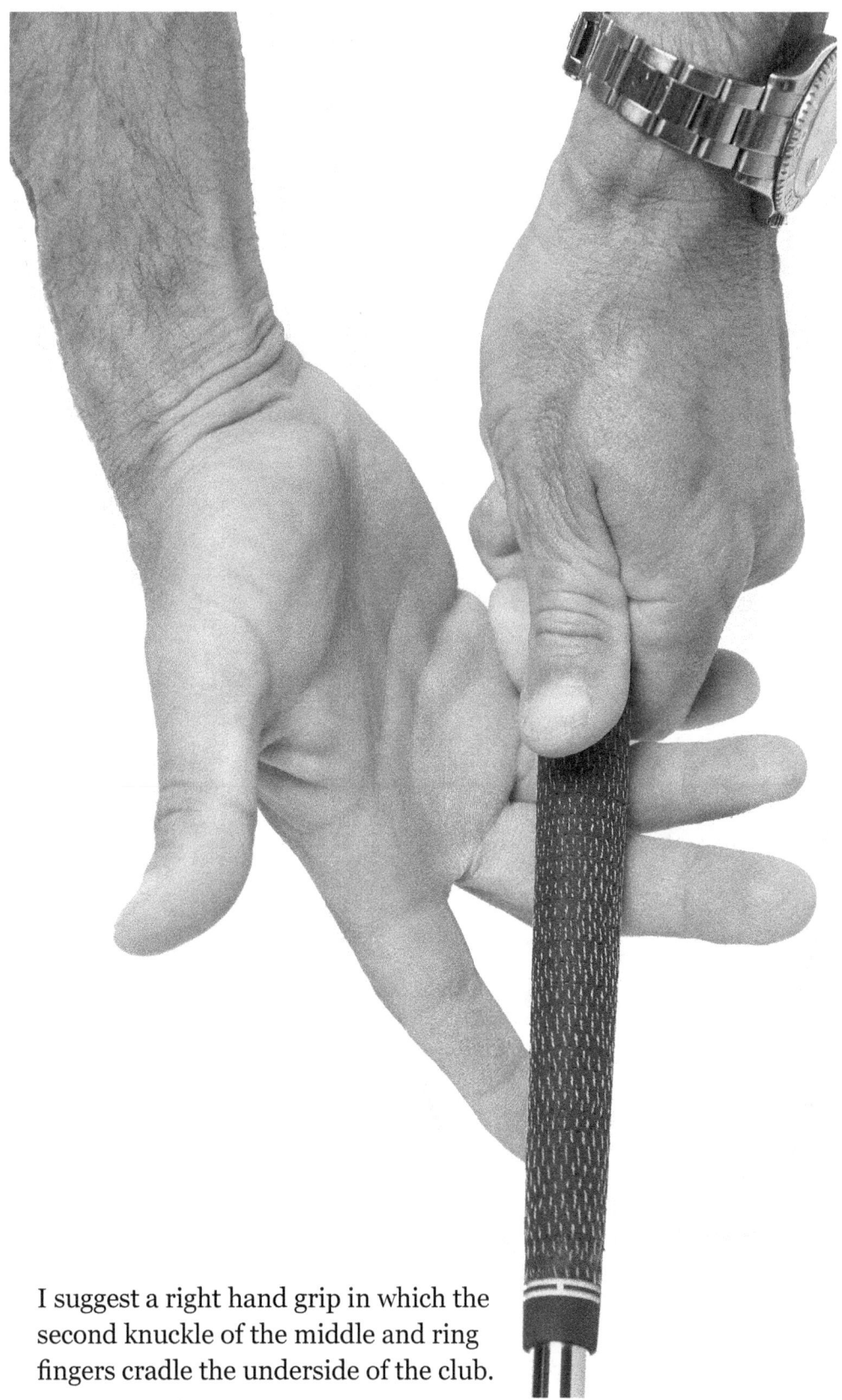

I suggest a right hand grip in which the second knuckle of the middle and ring fingers cradle the underside of the club.

THE GOLF SWING

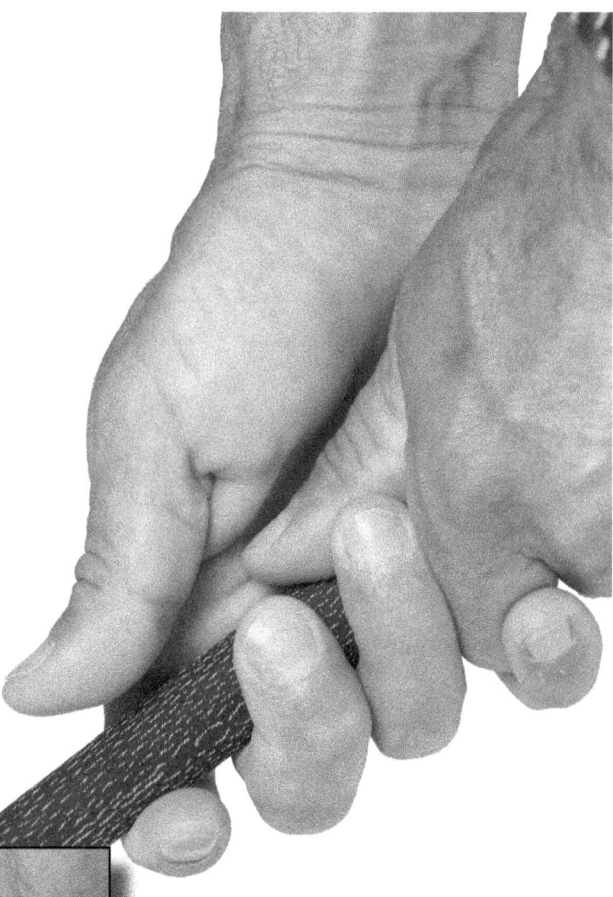

The lifeline of the right hand wraps over the top of the left thumb.

Finally, the index finger and right thumb are pinched together.

Step 1

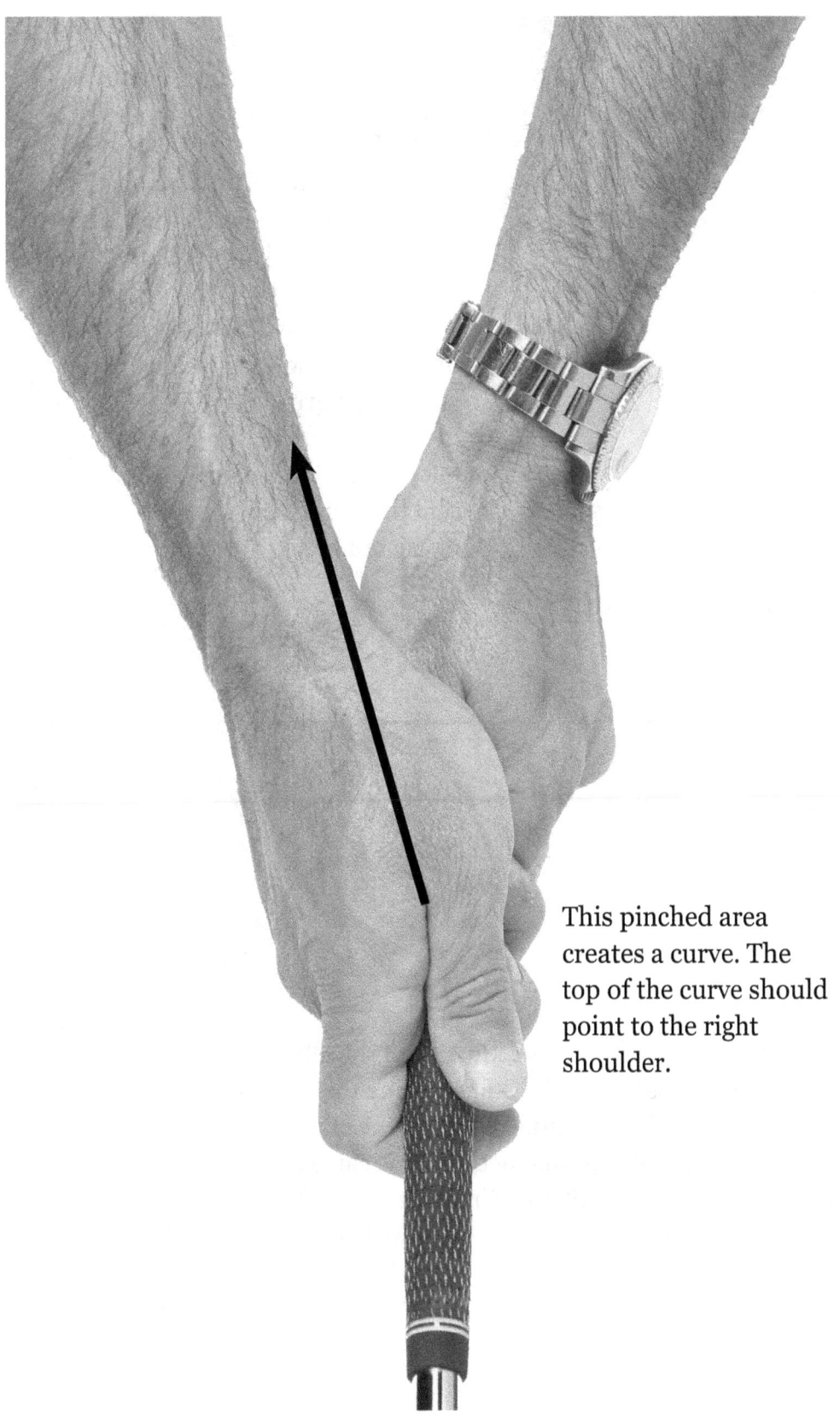

This pinched area creates a curve. The top of the curve should point to the right shoulder.

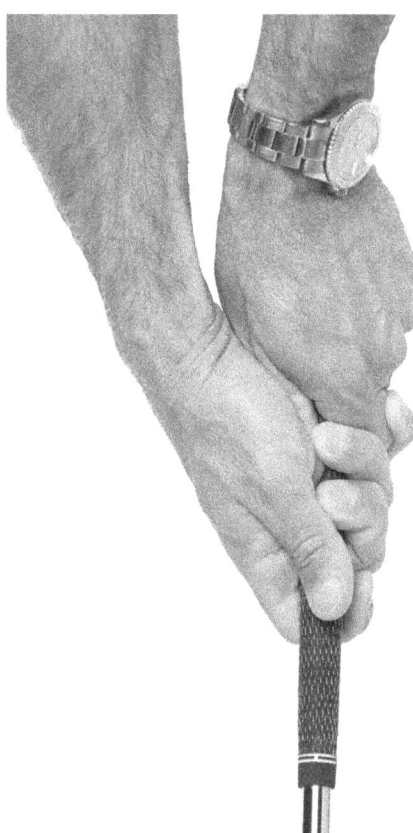

 **STRONG GRIP**

A "strong" grip is turned a bit to the right. This grip is fine if the golfer rotates their body exceptionally well.

If you see more than three knuckles of the left hand, that tends to be too strong of a grip. This type of grip will hit the ball too low and hook it to the left. Also, golfers using this grip will pull their chip shots and struggle out of the bunker.

 **WEAK GRIP**

If the golfer can only see one knuckle of the left hand, that grip is too weak. Golfers using this grip will have a difficult time squaring the club face without excessive hand action. This can lead to inconsistencies in loft and direction. The ball will tend to be hit weakly to the right with a high trajectory, and the impact will be too shallow.

Step 1

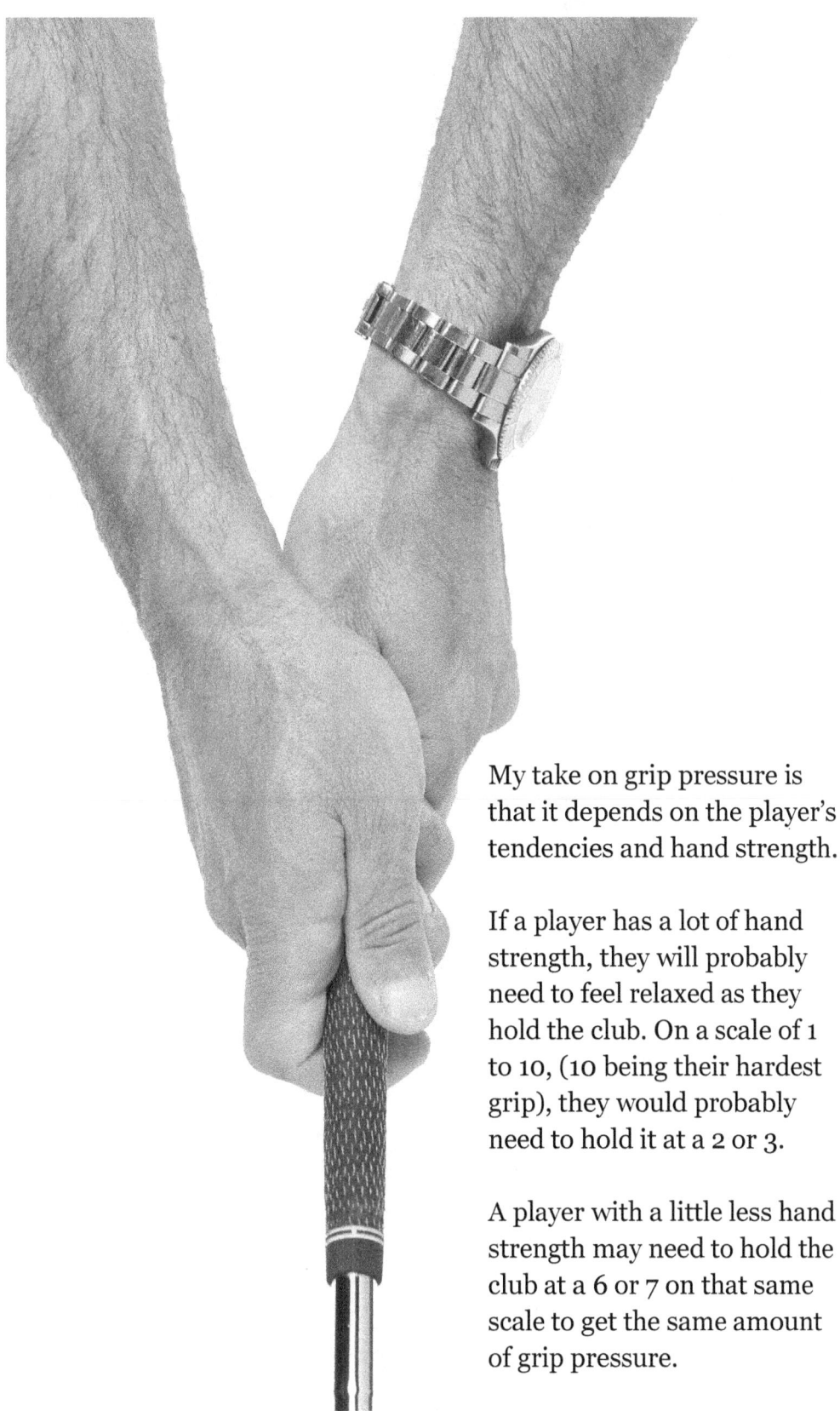

My take on grip pressure is that it depends on the player's tendencies and hand strength.

If a player has a lot of hand strength, they will probably need to feel relaxed as they hold the club. On a scale of 1 to 10, (10 being their hardest grip), they would probably need to hold it at a 2 or 3.

A player with a little less hand strength may need to hold the club at a 6 or 7 on that same scale to get the same amount of grip pressure.

The underside of the grip is personal preference. Great players throughout history have used different grips such as inter-locked, over-lapped, reverse-overlapped, and double-overlapped. They have even used the ten-finger grip.

But the majority of PGA Tour professionals use the over-lap grip seen here.

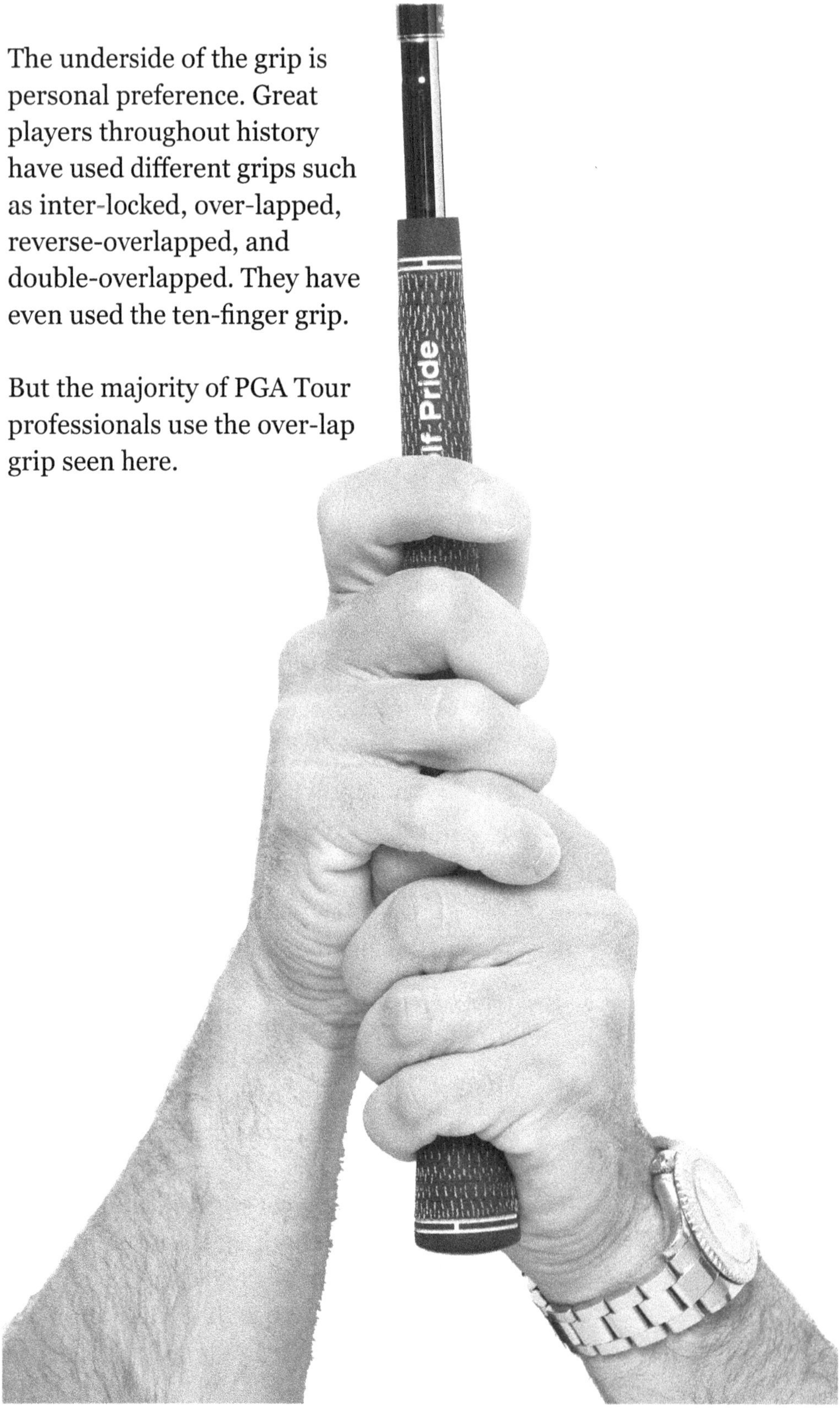

Step 1

Many ladies and juniors like the interlocking grip because their fingers are smaller and joints more flexible.

Experiment for yourself to see which grip feels secure and powerful.

Things to avoid when gripping the club:

1. Too loose of a grip: This takes away control. When you are holding on to an object flying around 100 mph, you need some grip pressure.

2. Hands too close together: This gives you the power of one hand instead of two.

3. Trying to "take the right hand out of it" by barely holding on with the right hand: This actually tends to backfire because a relaxed muscle is a fast muscle.

4. Changing the grip during the swing: If you start with it, finish with it.

5. Having the hands oppose each other: Learn a grip in which both hands tell the same story. No one has ever played great with one hand saying "fade" (weak) and the other saying "draw" (strong).

6. Regripping right before you pull the trigger: This usually causes pull hooks.

7. Interlocking your fingers too much: This causes lack of mobility in your wrists.

Step 1

The correct grip will give you the best chance to present the sweet spot of the club squarely to the ball.

The Golf Swing

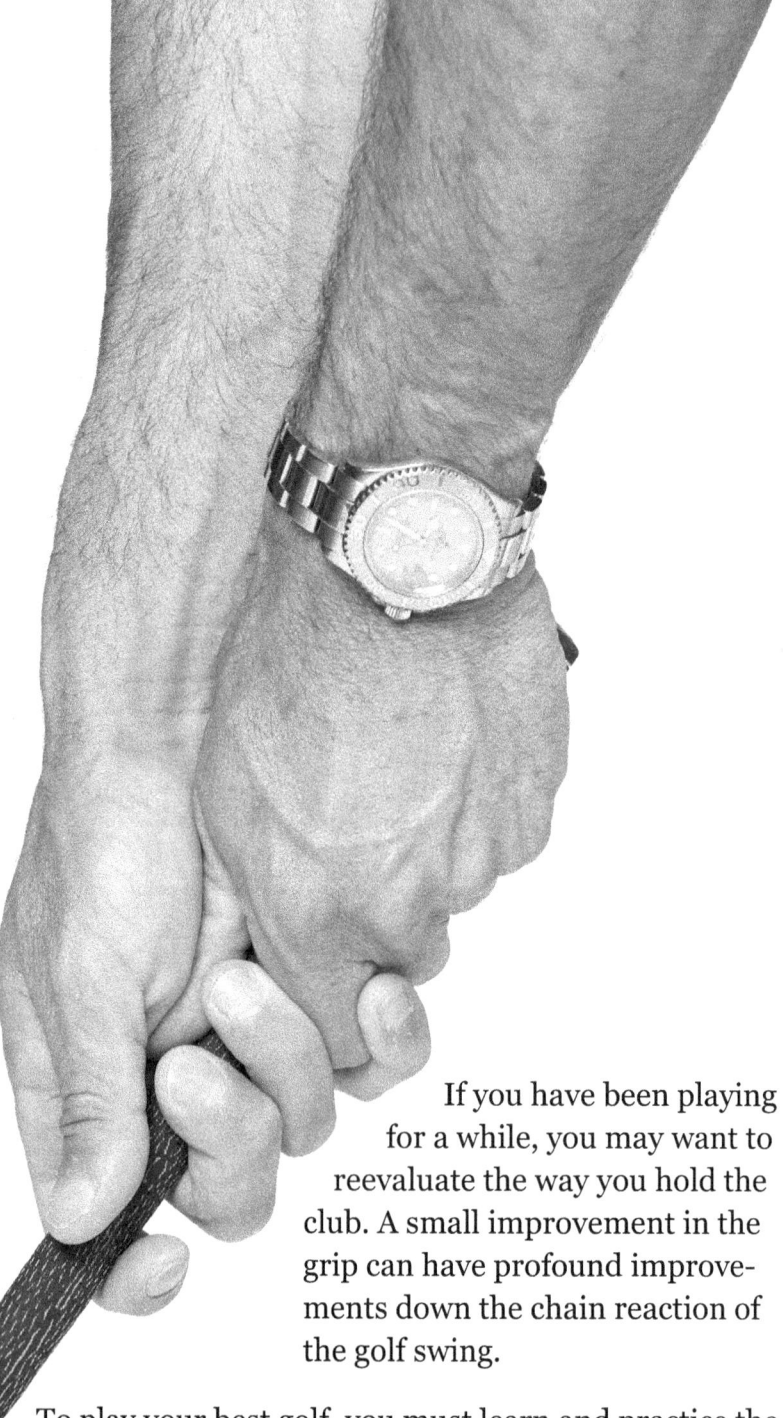

If you have been playing for a while, you may want to reevaluate the way you hold the club. A small improvement in the grip can have profound improvements down the chain reaction of the golf swing.

To play your best golf, you must learn and practice the correct grip. It may feel uncomfortable at first, but like my mentor, Hank Haney, says, "It is not about feeling comfortable; it is about feeling correct." All you have to do is stick with "correct" until it feels comfortable.

Step 1

S<small>ET</small>-U<small>P</small>

'The proper stance and posture enable the golfer to be perfectly balanced and poised throughout the swing. Only then will his legs, arms, and body be able to carry out their related assignments correctly"
—Ben Hogan

The Golf Swing

It is only through putting the body in the correct static position that the golfer is able to access the correct angles of the golf swing.

In addition to establishing the proper angles, a correct set-up accesses the correct muscles. It also positions you to move athletically.

The equipoise of being grounded and stable, combined with the sensation of being ready and lively, can only be obtained though the proper position at address.

The correct set-up depends somewhat on your physique. Each golfer has to find the right positioning based on the way their body is structured.

Those with shorter arms relative to the length of their torso, should stand a bit more bent over at address.

On the contrary, if a golfer has long arms and a shorter torso, they should stand somewhat taller.

These initial static angles will obviously effect the following dynamic angles of the swing.

Step 1

Aligning the eyes, shoulders, forearms, thighs, and feet parallel to the left of the target is the goal.

However, not all top-level golfers adhere to this maxim. About a third aim to the left of the target, a third to the right, and a third at the target.

I suggest starting out with the goal of being square to the target.

> *"Balance is the very beginning of any golf shot"*
> —Sam Snead

Back on Heels

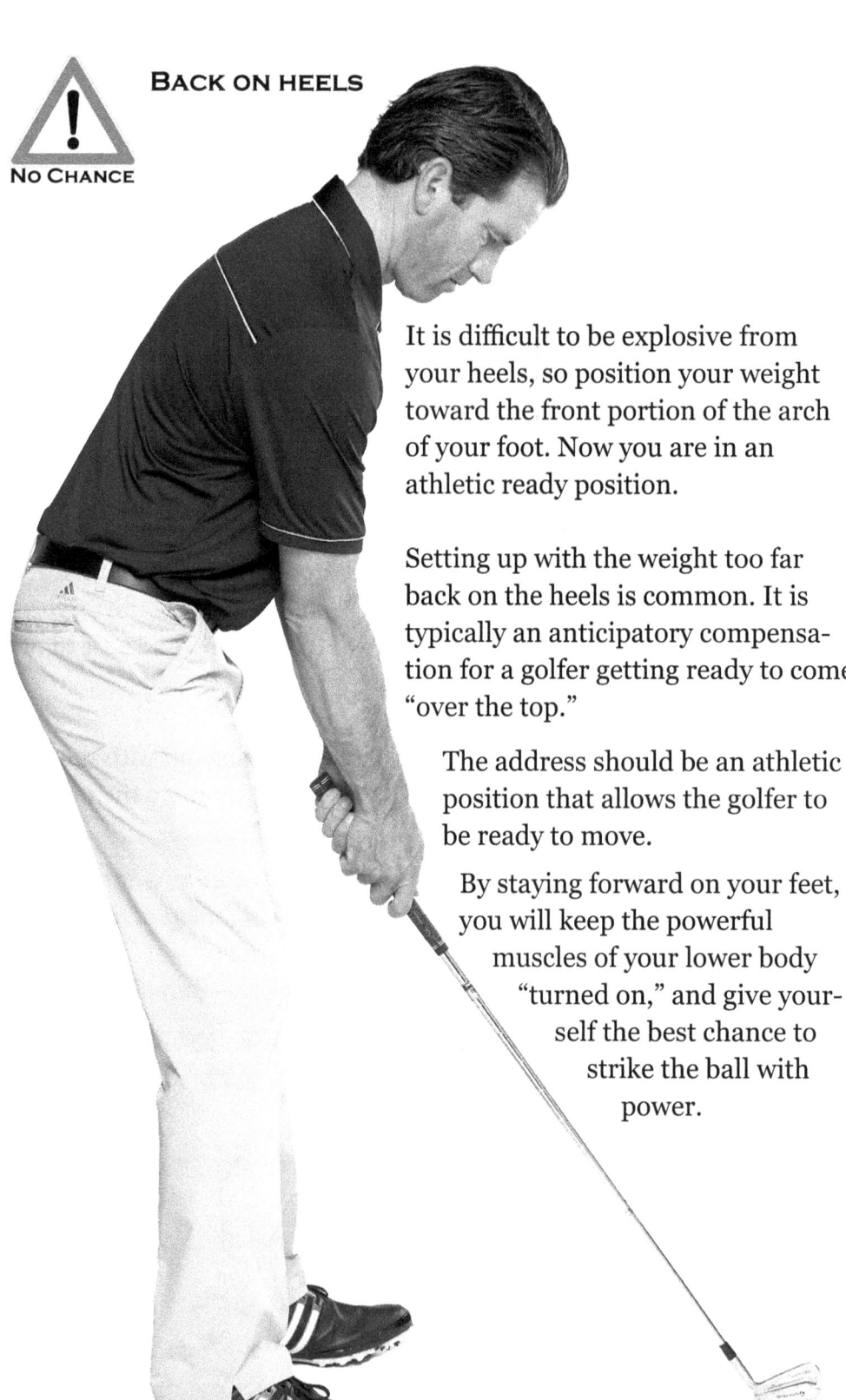

No Chance

It is difficult to be explosive from your heels, so position your weight toward the front portion of the arch of your foot. Now you are in an athletic ready position.

Setting up with the weight too far back on the heels is common. It is typically an anticipatory compensation for a golfer getting ready to come "over the top."

The address should be an athletic position that allows the golfer to be ready to move.

By staying forward on your feet, you will keep the powerful muscles of your lower body "turned on," and give yourself the best chance to strike the ball with power.

Step 1

For golfers that have a predictable curve (fade or draw) there is nothing wrong with angling your address lines to allow for the curve. Just make sure your shoulders, forearms, thighs, and feet are parallel to each other.

FADE SETUP

DRAW SETUP

NO CHANCE

It is good to have some active tension in your hands and arms, but most golfers carry too much tension in their forearms at address. Too much tension inhibits the golfer's ability to generate speed.

If you are going to err, err on the side of being too relaxed.

Because the right arm is below the left arm, the right shoulders should be noticeably below the left. This also pulls the spine slightly to the golfer's right. This is commonly referred to as secondary tilt.

From the face-on view with a shorter club, the left eye, center of the body, golf club, and ball are in a line.

As the club gets longer, the golfer should be set up more behind the ball. This set-up facilitates a shallow approach into the ball, which is optimal for longer clubs.

Some instructors advocate setting the hands slightly ahead of the ball at address. I do not follow this line of thinking. While it is good to have the shaft leaning forward at impact, a forward leaning shaft at address will tend to cause the takeaway to be rolled to the inside and out of position. Keep the true loft of the club present at address for your full swing, and save the shaft lean for impact.

The legs should have enough flex in them to allow for an athletic turn away from the ball, but not so much that the golfer loses stability.

Most weekend players tend to bend their knees too much. When the knees are bent too much, the upper body cannot bend properly from the hips. This sets the pivot on an improper angle, and makes it difficult for the golfer to swing the club on the proper path.

The golfer's posture should be tall enough to allow for a full and powerful turn, while bent over enough to give the arms room to swing freely.

Step 1

No Chance

Tilted Away from the Target

No Chance

Tilted Toward the Target

Correct Setup

Hands too High

No Chance

It is all but impossible to make a correct take away with the hands too high at address. Pay close attention to the angle between the hands and arms at address.

When the hands are too high at address, the forearms will tend to over rotate, and the club shaft will tend to be too flat with the face open. This is the prelude to the classic over-the-top mistake.

Correct

Step 1

Hands too Low

No Chance

Conversely, when the hands are set too low at address, it is difficult for the golfer to swing the club back correctly.

The torso is too bent over, putting additional stress on the spine and prohibiting a proper turn away from the ball.

Correct

THE GOLF SWING

NO CHANCE

POSTURE "TOO GOOD"

I have noticed some golfers have posture that is "too good," meaning they are actually concaving their lumbar spine. This posture turns the powerful core muscles off and can cause back injury.

The goal of a proper set-up is to start with your pelvis in a neutral position so your spine can rotate freely without causing injury.

CORRECT

Step 1

NO CHANCE

POSTURE TOO ROUNDED

The other type of posture that you want to avoid is being rounded to the point where your spine is in the shape of a "C." This posture will not allow your body to rotate properly, causing unnecessary sliding and lifting to create speed.

CORRECT

STEP 2

THE TAKE-AWAY
"The Dynamic Set-Up"

THE GOLF SWING

Now that your body is in the correct position, and your address is optimized for success, it's time to move the club face away from the ball and set up the swing.

Because the swing is a chain reaction, the takeaway sets up the rest of the swing. This is why I call it the "Dynamic Set-Up"; one element sets up the next element, all the way through the next four steps.

Many people have the misconception that the take away is one piece. While I would rather "one-piece" than "all pieces out of position," the takeaway is not quite one piece.

The club should move away from the ball in three dimensions:

- In
- Up
- Back

Blending these three directions in one gradual motion is the trick to the proper takeaway. What actually occurs is the wrists hinge, the arms swing back, and the body turns.

A quick note about the speed of the takeaway.
I often see golfers who look as though they are just trying to get the takeaway over with. They sling the club back so fast, it is difficult for them to remain in rhythm. When the golfer swings the club back quickly, they usually swing down slowly and lose power.

The takeaway should be the slowest part of the swing, with the club increasing in speed as it goes back. That is not to say that the takeaway must be slow; it just must be in rhythm with the overall swing. A smooth takeaway will help to keep your entire swing in tempo.

During the start of the takeaway, the club face stays square to the arc. When it is parallel to the ground, the club shaft should also be parallel to where you are trying to go. This is a great checkpoint that is easy to recall.

The wrist hinge should be a gradual motion that starts at the beginning, and gradually completes at the top of the backswing. When you are half-way into the backswing, your wrists should be about 50% hinged. And when you are done with your backswing, the wrists should be fully hinged.

As the wrists hinge up, the arms swing back and away from the target, creating some width in the backswing. At the same time, your hips begin to turn gradually while trying to maintain your posture as you rotate into the takeaway. The right leg should gradually decrease its flex, and the left leg should gradually increase the flex, allowing the hips to turn freely.

> *"The golf swing is action and reaction"*
> —John Jacobs

THE GOLF SWING

Keep your clubhead "in front" of you during the takeaway.

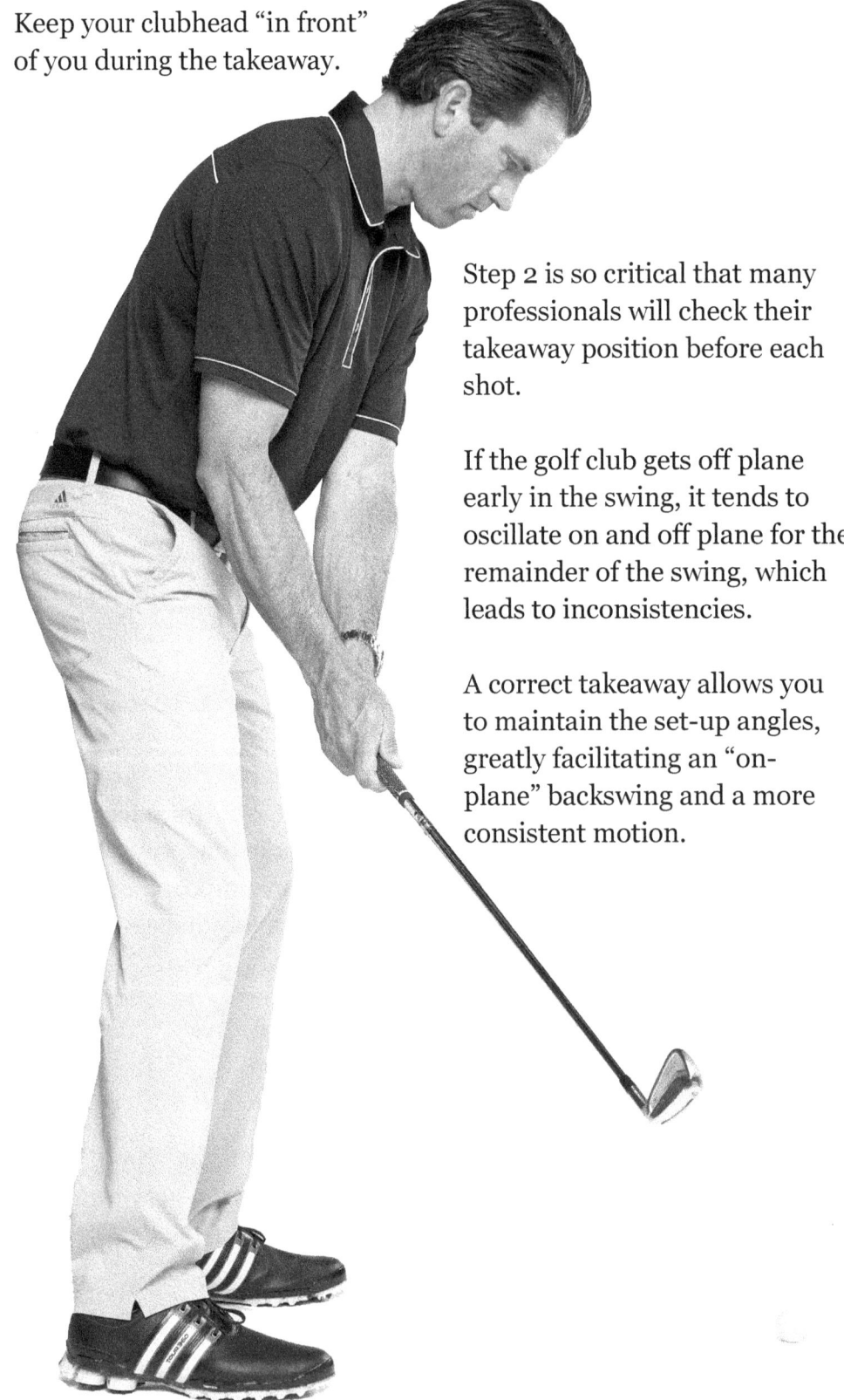

Step 2 is so critical that many professionals will check their takeaway position before each shot.

If the golf club gets off plane early in the swing, it tends to oscillate on and off plane for the remainder of the swing, which leads to inconsistencies.

A correct takeaway allows you to maintain the set-up angles, greatly facilitating an "on-plane" backswing and a more consistent motion.

Step 2

In the takeaway of the **Six Step Swing**, the club passes through a point that is parallel to the ground and parallel to the target line. This is a swing "landmark" that has stood the test of time. It is a position that is easy to train and recall because it can be perceived without a mirror, video, 3D analyzing machine, launch monitor, etc.

THE GOLF SWING

You can train yourself to make a correct takeaway.

Place a club on the ground, parallel to the target line, as a reference.

Midway through the backswing, the club should be parallel to the club on the ground. Your shoulders, arms, and hands should work together smoothly.

From this position, it is relatively easy to continue swinging the club into position at the top of the backswing.

Step 2

The second half of the backswing is a continuation of the good angles that were created in the takeaway.

The body keeps pivoting as the shoulders turn and the arms reach back to the top of the swing. During that time, the wrists are hinging so when you get to the top of your swing, you've got 100% of your wrist hinge. This loading of the wrists is stored power that will be released into the back of the ball.

The Golf Swing

⚠ NO CHANCE

Avoid rolling the club flat in the take-away. This is a difficult mistake to recover from.

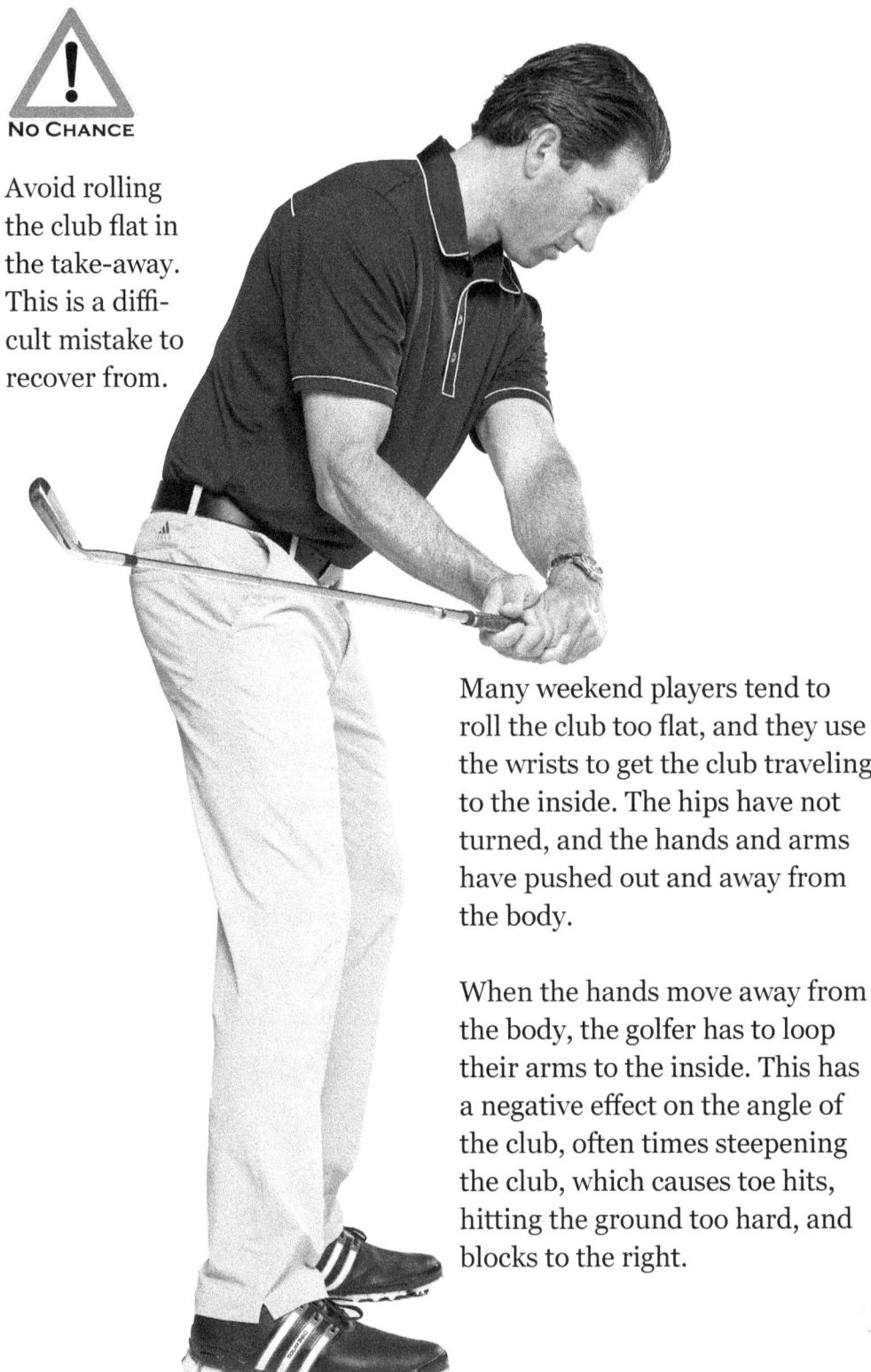

Many weekend players tend to roll the club too flat, and they use the wrists to get the club traveling to the inside. The hips have not turned, and the hands and arms have pushed out and away from the body.

When the hands move away from the body, the golfer has to loop their arms to the inside. This has a negative effect on the angle of the club, often times steepening the club, which causes toe hits, hitting the ground too hard, and blocks to the right.

Step 2

Correct

TOP OF THE SWING
"The Exchange"

THE GOLF SWING

There is a misconception that the backswing ends at a defined point, and the downswing starts at a defined point. The reality is that the lines between the backswing and the downswing are blurred. The great instructor, Jim Hardy told me once that if the backswing is "one," the downswing is "three," and what happens in between is "two," or what I call the "exchange."

During the exchange, the club should be on plane. If the club is short of parallel to the ground, it will point to the left of the target. If it is parallel to the ground, then it will be parallel to the target line.

And if the club were to swing past parallel, it will point to the right of the target.

"Quiet head in the backswing. Quiet feet in the downswing."
—Peter Kostis

Step 3

During the backswing, the shaft should ride along the original "shaft plane" angle, and then remain parallel as the arms rise up slightly above the shoulders.

The Golf Swing

Once the club starts down toward the ball, the golfer has about 0.3 seconds before impact. That does not leave a lot of time for corrections to take place. This is why it is so important for the golfer to have the club face square at the top.

As the golfer is winding into the backswing, their head should remain quiet, their eyes should stay level, and their shoulders should turn at right angles to their posture.

The lower body acts as a point of stability, only turning half as much as the upper body. It gives the upper body something to coil against.

The right leg straightens as the left leg increases knee flex. The left knee should be pointing slightly behind the ball.

Step 3

Just before the club starts down, the thighs, glutes, and core are activated. There is a tremendous amount of tension built into the body at this point, so much so that, as the golfer approaches the top of the backswing, their body should start down just fractionally before the club reaches its maximum point. This adds additional pressure and tension on the muscles of the back, core, and lower body, giving the golfer access to even more power that can be delivered into the back of the ball.

The hips stay right underneath the shoulders as the torso rotates around, creating a coiled, powerful pivot.

Tilted eyes / Reverse pivot

No Chance

A good player keeps their eye line quiet during the course of the swing. The higher the handicap, the more the eyes tend to dance around, tilt, and rotate.

It is very important that the golfer keeps their eyes level to the horizon as they work their way into the backswing. Since the ball is not moving, there is no need for the golfer to change their proximity to the ball.

When the eyes stay level to the ground, the golfer has an accurate representation of what square really is. This allows the club to return consistently to the ball.

If the golfer tilts their eyes, they either crash down into the ball in too steep of an angle, or they over-recover in a "rocking and blocking" fashion that sends the ball sailing right.

Step 3

During the backswing, the hands should progress to the inside as the body pivots, while simultaneously traveling up and away from the ground. This allows the golfer to attack the ball powerfully from the inside.

Wrist Cup

Assuming a neutral grip, the left wrist should be flat at the top of the swing. If you cup the left wrist, you are also opening the club face. When the face is open at the top of the swing, the golfer will have a tendency to have over active hands.

A flat left wrist will help you square the club face and it will deliver a more powerful loft to the back of the golf ball.

Step 3

During the backswing, the right arm gradually bends until it is approximately at a 90-degree angle. This provides the width needed to maintain proper swing arc, which equals maximum power.

90°

No Chance

Many golfers have too much right arm flex at the top of their backswing. This causes both elbows to break down too much, preventing the golfer from hinging the wrist properly.

When the right elbow breaks down, the swing becomes too narrow. As the golfer tries to find the correct width in the downswing, they release the club in a way that is out of sequence. This type of release makes it difficult to create solid ball-turf contact.

Step 3

NO CHANCE

When a player starts down with a rotary motion and no forward hip motion, the arms tend to get too far over the top the plane. When this happens, the club comes into the ball on too steep of an angle. To get the club head to hit the back of the ball, the body has to slow down and the hands and arms end up flipping through impact. This causes severe mis-hits, occasional pull-hooks, or powerless slices to the right.

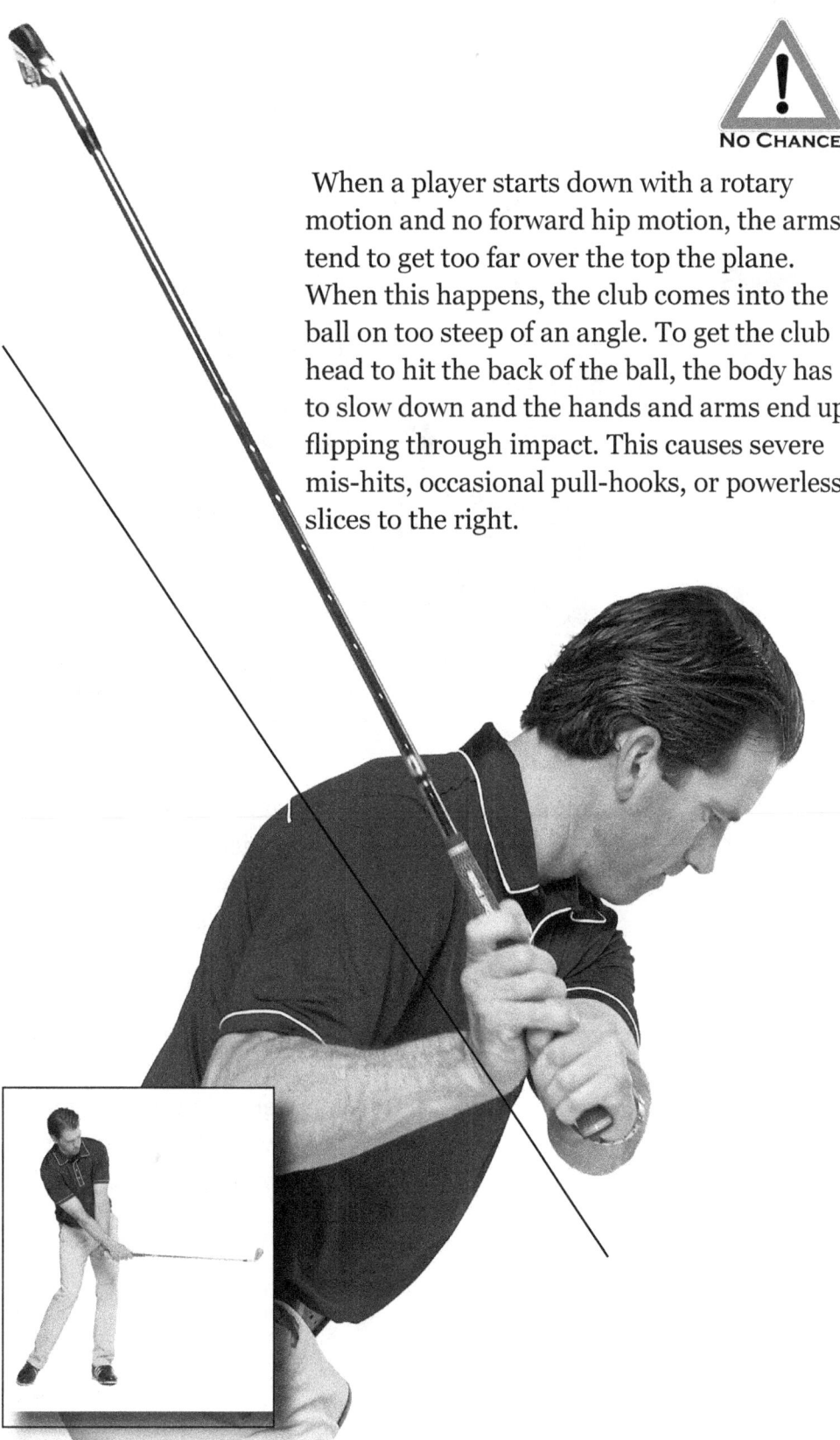

The downswing is initiated by transferring the weight from the right foot to the left foot.

This initiates the sequence in which the golfer uses their body as a bull-whip. The hips accelerate first, then the shoulders, arms, hands, the shaft, and eventually the sweet spot of the club head.

A note about footwork
As the golfer starts down, the left foot grips the ground creating an anchor point around which the body can rotate. You don't want to jump off the ground or have your feet leave the ground; that tends to cause an overuse of the hands and an inconsistency in the bottom of the swing. This also creates a lot of thin shots.

As the golfer starts down, the weight goes mainly on the left foot, placing a tremendous amount of pressure into the ground.

Pre-Impact
"The Gathering Storm"

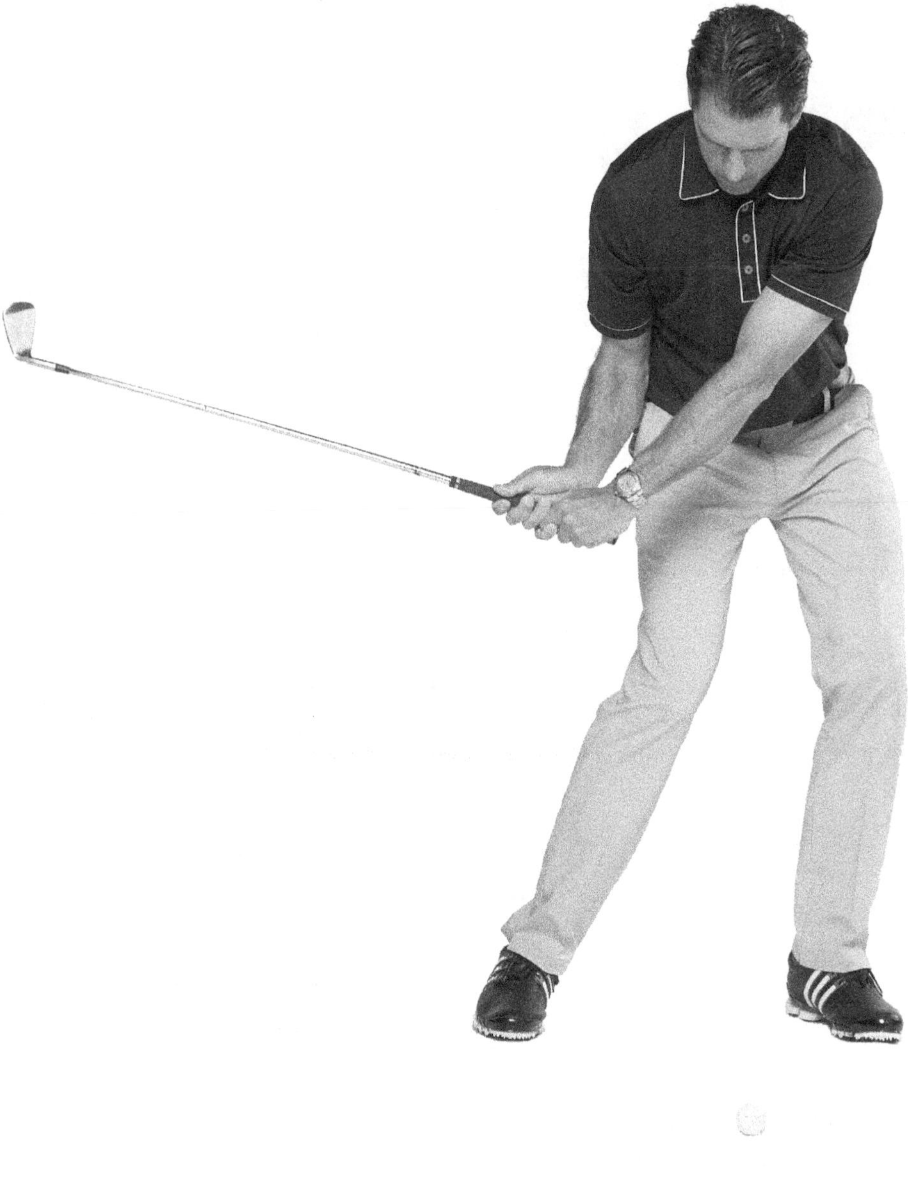

The Golf Swing

As the golfer moves into the downswing, the clubhead travels down the proper plane as the body turns up.

The shoulders should almost be parallel to the target line.

The back of the right wrist has a little bit of a bend to it. The wrists still have plenty of hinge.

The hips are open to the target line.

If you hold the body back too much, you create a hook. If you rotate the body too fast, you create a fade.

Every golfer's body will have a slightly different look at this point based on their flexibility. But that doesn't mean that this is not a great checkpoint. Be aware of what your body will allow you to do.

Step 4

When the club is parallel to the ground and parallel to the target line, the body is working around to the left.

The wrists have started to release, but they still have plenty of hinge left to deliver a powerful crack-of-the-whip through the ball.

As the club head swings into impact, it travels along the original shaft angle.

A good player will tend to have a slight bump forward with their hips and enough lateral motion to transfer the weight from the right foot to the left foot. This transfer of weight gives the hands and arms time to travel down enough from the inside so the player can get a solid strike on the golf ball.

The golf swing, at it's essence, is simply cracking a whip around an axis on a specific angle.

Through impact, the golf club should be leaning slightly forward to varying degrees. While the driver shouldn't have much shaft lean at impact, the irons should have up to ten degrees of shaft lean. This "lean" insures the pinching motion necessary to create clean contact with the ball. The less loft on the golf club, the less it should be leaning forward.

There is also a wide zone of acceptance for shaft lean at impact based on the angle of attack and club head speed. The higher the club head speed, the more important the shaft lean becomes to keep the spin rate and launch angle from getting too high. A high-spinning ball is difficult to control.

Experiment to find out how much shaft lean produces your best shots.

The Golf Swing

No Chance — In Step 4, if your eyes tilt to the right in the downswing, the club will tend to drop too much from the inside, and the follow-through will extend out to the right. This is a mistake that many good golfers have, even some tour players.

This problem tends to have a negative effect on the downswing, moving the bottom of the swing behind the ball. This causes fat and thin shots. It also makes it more difficult for the body to turn through the shot.

This mistake tends to put a tremendous amount of pressure on your neck and upper back. The cumulative effect can cause injury.

Step 4

If the eyes tilt to the left, the swing will typically get angled too far over-the-top, causing pulls and slices.

NO CHANCE

Tilting the eyes is usually the first domino to fall in a reverse pivot. The hips slide out from under the shoulders and the golfer is in no position to make an on-plane downswing. This also causes additional stress on the neck and back.

CORRECT

Post Impact
"Fully Extended"

There is a point in the swing where the club catches up to the hands, arms, torso, and lower body. Everything is lined up at a moment of full extension. Chuck Cook, the renowned golf instructor, defines this as "a moment of culminating forces."

This is the point where the angles of the hips and shoulders line up, both arms are extended straight, the club face is square to the arc, and the club is on plane.

The left leg should be in the process of straightening, and the hips should be thrusting up for additional power.

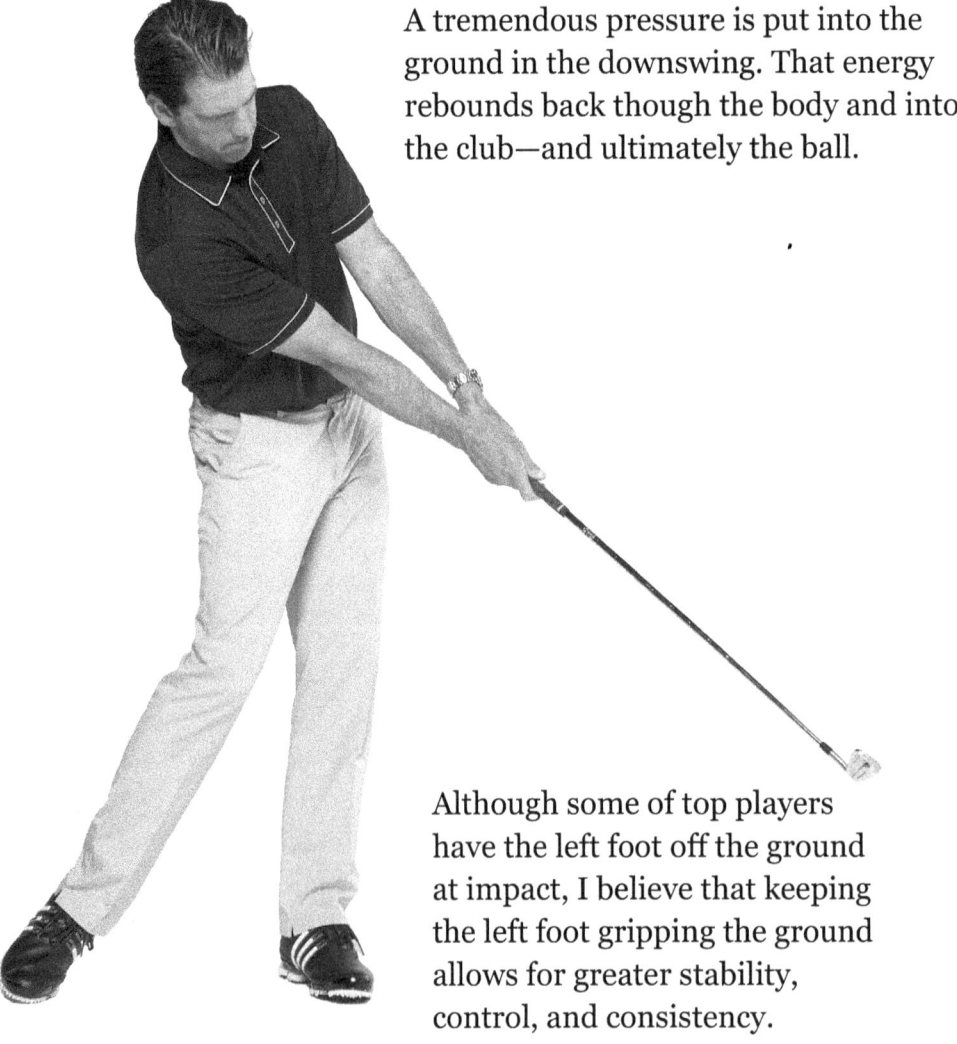

A tremendous pressure is put into the ground in the downswing. That energy rebounds back though the body and into the club—and ultimately the ball.

Although some of top players have the left foot off the ground at impact, I believe that keeping the left foot gripping the ground allows for greater stability, control, and consistency.

Step 5

SCOOPING

The high-handicap player tends to stop their body and throw the club head at the ball. This causes their lead hand to collapse through impact. This is typically a result of a steep angle coming into the ball. In a last-ditch attempt to shallow the club before it strikes the ball, the golfer shuts down any rotation or forward movement.

⚠️ **NO CHANCE**

This tends to present different amounts of loft to the golf ball, causing the ball to fly in different distances.

Next, it tends to make it very difficult to get the leading edge to pinch underneath the golf ball.

It also increases the closing effect of the club face. This causes the ball to start left of your intended line, and it usually curves farther left.

OVER-THE-TOP

It also creates power loss because, instead of cracking the whip properly through the ball and extending through the target line, the golf club is simply flipped; the energy does not get transferred properly into the back of the golf ball.

⚠ No Chance

A common problem is the body changing its angles as the club is swinging into the ball. The usual cause of this is the club swinging on too steep of an angle during the downswing.

When the golfer changes posture, the trailing hip works into the area that was meant for the free swinging of the hands and arms. Since there is little room for the arms to swing from the inside, they will tend to hit from the outside. This is a recipe for pulls and slices (and the occasional shank!).

Because of this steep angle, the club would tend to hit the ground too hard if the golfer stayed in this posture. In an attempt to shallow out the impact, the golfer usually shortens their arms (chicken wing) or jumps up on their toes, or a combination of both.

Step 5

No Chance

Jumping up on the toes, the golfer will tend to hit "thin" shots. In addition, the right leg moves into the space that the hands and arms need to deliver the club properly into the back of the ball.

THE GOLF SWING

The proper way to swing the club into the ball is to keep the dynamic angles of the body intact as the body is rotating through impact. This allows for a more consistent delivery of the golf club.

Step 5

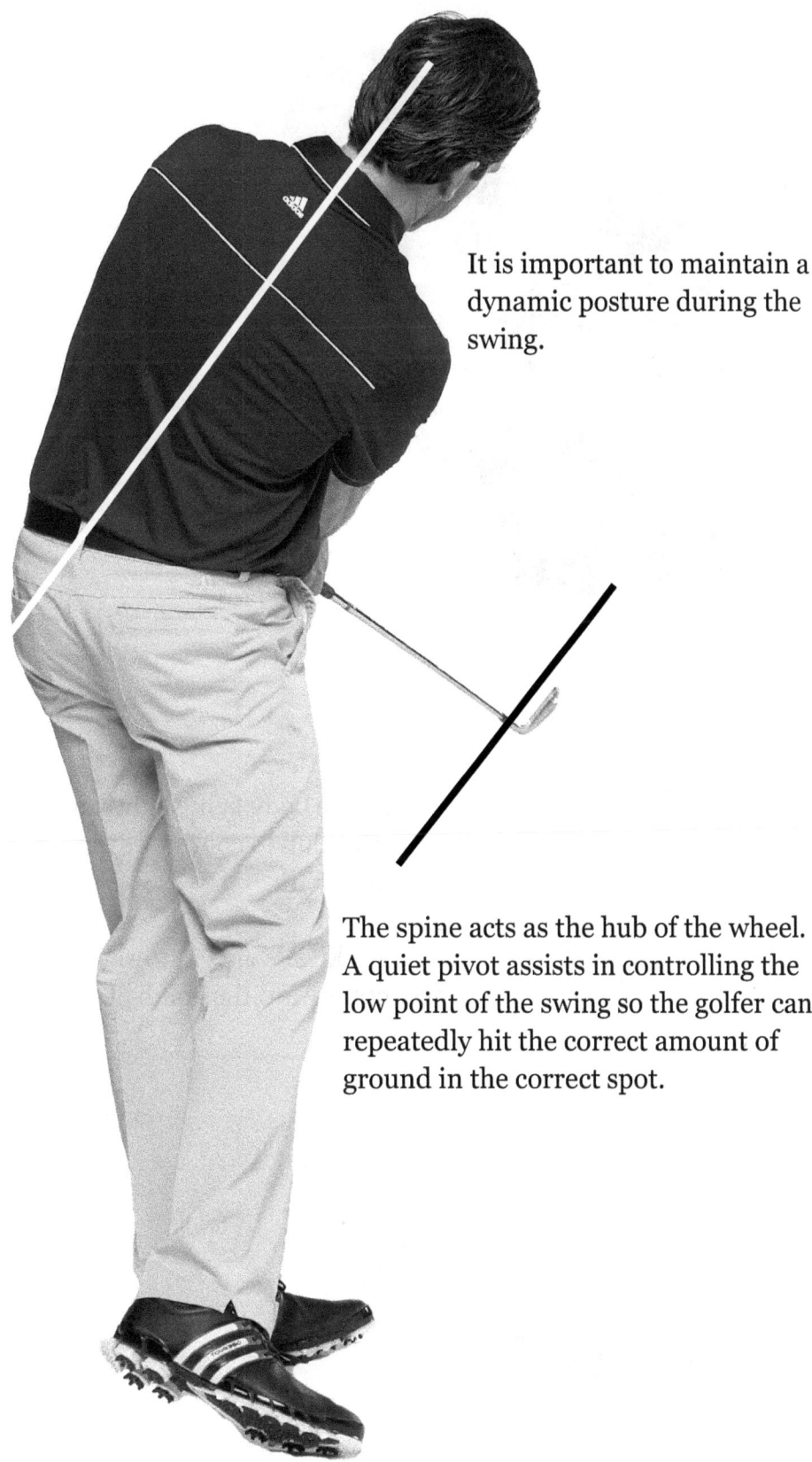

It is important to maintain a dynamic posture during the swing.

The spine acts as the hub of the wheel. A quiet pivot assists in controlling the low point of the swing so the golfer can repeatedly hit the correct amount of ground in the correct spot.

The Golf Swing

Keeping the body bent slightly to the right allows the club to continue swinging on the proper path.

The right knee works in toward the left knee, not toward the golf ball.

Step 5

After impact, the club should pass through a point where it is in-line with your left arm. You want your left wrist flat and both arms straight so that the club face is square to the "path" of the swing. And your weight should be on your left foot with your right heel slightly off the ground.

The Golf Swing

Punch Drill A great drill for creating proper impact is the Punch Drill. It combines the start of the swing with the sensation of a correct impact. Use a lofted club and hit some balls with a small swing.

Place your feet slightly open to the target line and closer together than normal. You want the outside of your feet even with the outside of your shoulders.

Take the club back far enough so you can create some speed in the downswing.

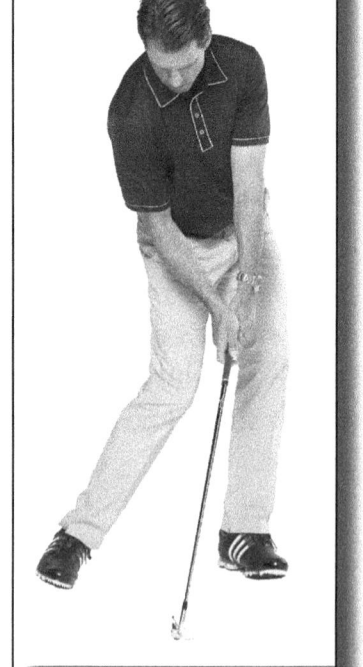

As you hit through the ball, feel the shaft leaning forward. Show the ball who's the boss; don't be afraid to give it a decisive hit.

Step 5

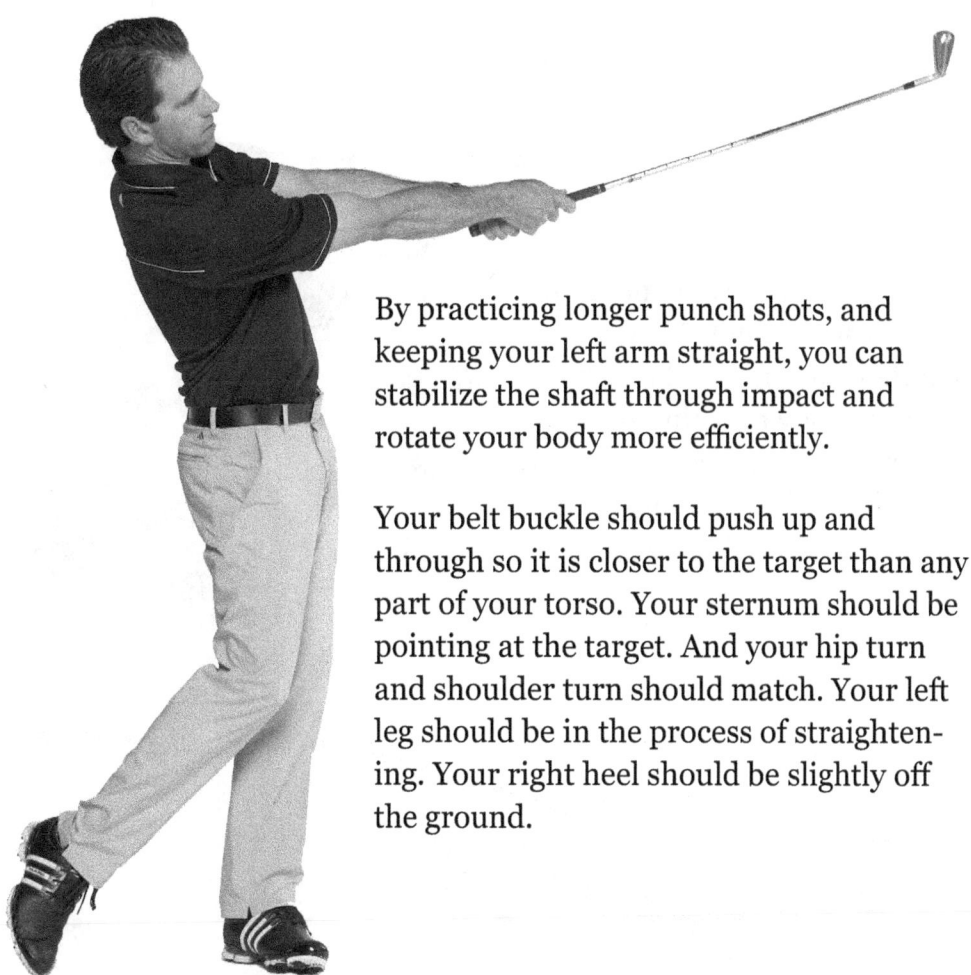

By practicing longer punch shots, and keeping your left arm straight, you can stabilize the shaft through impact and rotate your body more efficiently.

Your belt buckle should push up and through so it is closer to the target than any part of your torso. Your sternum should be pointing at the target. And your hip turn and shoulder turn should match. Your left leg should be in the process of straightening. Your right heel should be slightly off the ground.

Hitting the ball with the punch drill will allow you to work on "cracking the whip" in an efficient way while giving you the sensation of compressing the ball. Often the golfer is surprised by how far the ball goes with such a small swing. This is why, when you see players hitting the ball really straight, it is usually more of a "punchy" motion, as opposed to a full-blooded lash at the ball. They give up a few yards to gain control of their game.

THE GOLF SWING

Many golfers have a tendency to stay down to a fault. They've heard that they are supposed to keep their head down. Thinking about keeping your head down interferes with your ability to rotate all the way through the shot.

Focusing too much on "staying down" causes chunks and hooks. The golfer hits the ground too hard. Also, it decreases the club head speed because keeping the head down interferes with the body's ability to rotate in an aggressive manner.

Step 5

If you feel that you are "staying down" to a fault, hit a few shots practicing "looking off" the ball.

One of the trends I have noticed in recent years on the PGA Tour is more players are "looking off" the ball. This means that they are literally not even looking at the golf ball when they strike it. Their eyes are looking toward the target before contact.

Now, I am not suggesting that you take it to that extreme, but I will say that I would prefer that mistake over getting stuck looking at the ground too long.

The correct release is to allow the eyes to rotate with the chest so there is less stress on the neck and it is easier to get through the shot.

When the first steps of the swing are done correctly, the post impact position feels virtually automatic. You will feel like the ball just gets in the way as you breeze through impact!

Step 5

Follow Through
"Catching the Speed"

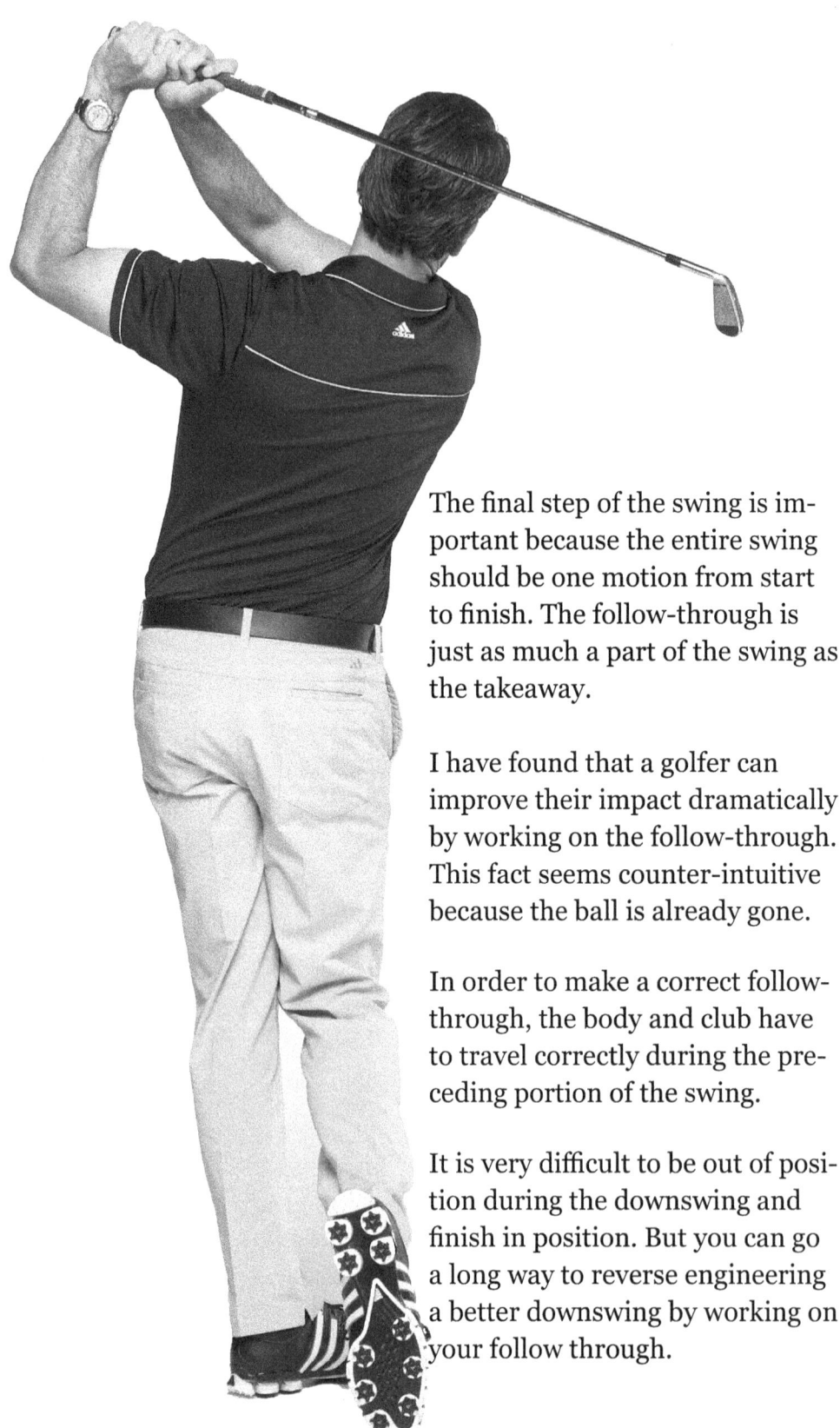

The final step of the swing is important because the entire swing should be one motion from start to finish. The follow-through is just as much a part of the swing as the takeaway.

I have found that a golfer can improve their impact dramatically by working on the follow-through. This fact seems counter-intuitive because the ball is already gone.

In order to make a correct follow-through, the body and club have to travel correctly during the preceding portion of the swing.

It is very difficult to be out of position during the downswing and finish in position. But you can go a long way to reverse engineering a better downswing by working on your follow through.

Step 6

The best players tend to be the best decelerators. They have the ability to catch the speed of their swing in a way that allows them to stay balanced and poised at the finish.

The torso should rotate through just left of the target. The belt buckle, ideally, should point at the target. Virtually all of your weight should be on the outside of the left foot towards the heel. At this point, the right foot simply becomes a kickstand because it has such a small amount of weight on it.

The Golf Swing

During the follow-though, the shaft should swing right on plane before relaxing to a balanced finish.

The swing should be symmetrical so the right arm during the follow through mirrors the left arm in the backswing.

Step 6

If the hands finish too low and to the left, the golfer will tend to hit pulls and fades.

When the hands finish too high and out to the right, the golfer will tend to hit pushes and hooks.

The Golf Swing

No Chance

When a player follows through, they sometimes tend to over rotate their body to the left. This makes their sternum face well left of the target.

As the body rotates harder to the left, it makes the path move more to the left. This is great for reducing a hook, but most golfers fight a slice, and the over-rotated finish tends to aggravate a slice.

In an attempt to keep the ball from flying more to the right many golfers tend to over rotate more and more to the left. This creates a vicious circle that creates a myriad of mistakes from shanks to hard pulls to slices.

Step 6

No Chance

Conversely, when a player does not turn their body through enough, their sternum will actually face to the right of the target. This causes the path to be too much from in to out, and causes the hands to become over-active through impact.

This is a formula for a hook. The more the ball hooks to the left, the more the golfer is afraid to turn through to the left. This only aggravates the hook spin on the ball, creating the opposite vicious circle, of fat and thin shots, hooks, and the occasional block to the right.

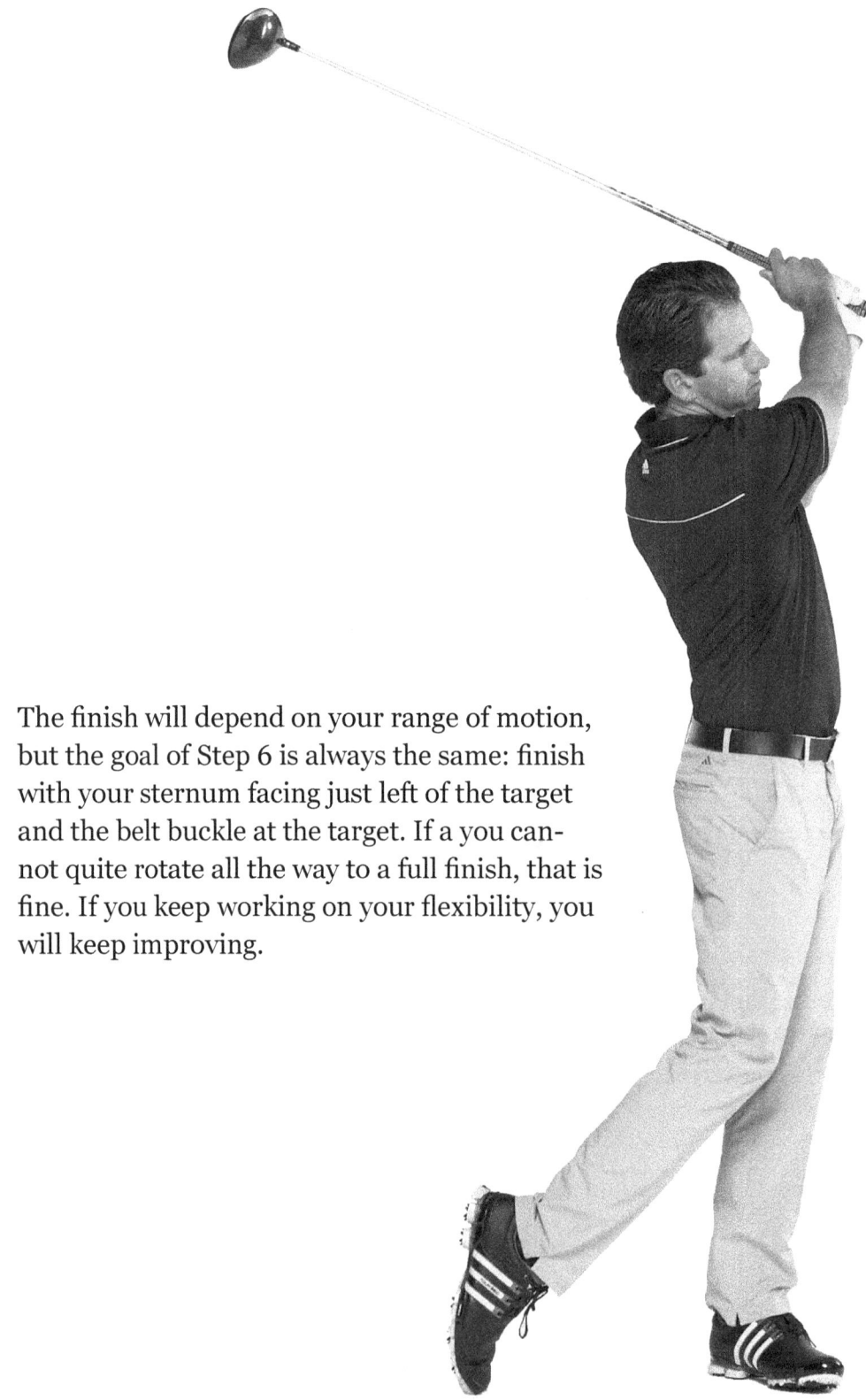

The finish will depend on your range of motion, but the goal of Step 6 is always the same: finish with your sternum facing just left of the target and the belt buckle at the target. If a you cannot quite rotate all the way to a full finish, that is fine. If you keep working on your flexibility, you will keep improving.

In Step 6, the eyes are up and following the ball. The neck is in line with the rest of the spine, which has some tilt to the right. The upper body should have some tilt away from the target because the hips have thrusted toward the target, creating a small "reverse C" with the body. Again, this is dependent on the golfers flexibility.

During a proper follow-through, the sequence of the swing is reversed. The hips complete their movement first, then the shoulders, arms, and then finally the hands and club.

This reversing of the sequence is what allows the club to decelerate after impact. The golfer gradually absorbs the power of the swing, finishing poised and in balance, giving the swing an effortless look.

The Golf Swing

The club has traveled all the way around and is across the back of your eye line in the finished position. Your elbows are relaxed. The hands are supporting the club and are up and away from the shoulders. The upper body is tipped slightly to the right, and the left hip is the farthest point to the left.

Step 6

The golfer is poised and in perfect balance with an effortless look to their finish.

The right leg should be relaxed. It has pivoted up and away so that it is almost perpendicular to the ground.

The left leg is now straight because it has thrusted up during impact and follow-through.

Conclusion

I have always felt fortunate to have golf in my life. It is a constant challenge and endless study. The more you know about the game, the more doors open for additional knowledge.

That being said, I am always trying to define the golf swing in the fewest number of principles. In this book, I have tried to lay the plan for a swing that is as simple as possible. These 6 Steps have been distilled from all the information I have absorbed over 20 years of teaching golf. I have closely observed great instructors like Hank Haney, John Jacobs, Butch Harmon, and Jim Hardy, to name a few. I've seen what they have done to achieve remarkable results with their students. I've tried to reproduce that in the 6 Step Swing.

The 6 Steps that I am sharing with you have been time-tested and tournament-tested. Some of these ideas date back to instructional books written in the 1800s, and have been validated by the latest 3D diagnostic equipment. They will help you take your game to the next level and beyond.

By breaking the swing down into manageable pieces, I believe anyone can learn a great swing. If you take your time and get a vivid picture of these 6 Steps, you will be able to blend them into your best swing.

STEP 1

The most important part of the golf swing is not the swing at all; it is the set-up. If the golfer can't get the static part correct, they won't be able to execute the dynamic part correctly. So much of the swing is about angle creation and retention. This is why the best players work on their set-up every day. It is the first place they look when they start hitting the ball poorly because it is the root of most swing flaws. The best way to work on your set-up is with a mirror. You can see if your alignments are parallel and check your posture. Although it is difficult to swing like a pro, it is entirely possible for the average person to set up like a pro.

STEP 2

The takeaway is the gateway to a good swing. If you mess up the start of your swing, you spend the rest of the swing trying to make up for it. So make sure that you are maintaining a proper takeaway. Use a mirror to see that the club is passing through a point that is parallel to the ground and parallel to the target line.

Step 3

The top of the backswing and the start of the downswing are blended together. In theory, there is no specific "top of the backswing" because by the time the club is all the way back, the hips are already on their way into the downswing. I believe if the club is delivered to the top correctly, it becomes easier to start down correctly.

Step 4

As a check point for the middle of the downswing, make sure the club is parallel to the ground and parallel the target line simultaneously. This will allow the club to be delivered from the inside on a shallow angle, transferring the speed of the club into the back of the ball. You want to feel your feet gripping the ground and torquing your body around to the left. This rotation creates a tremendous amount of speed. When you look down at your knees you should see that they are open (angled left of the target line). Your right arm should still have a bit of a bend to it and your wrist should still have plenty of hinge. These angles are storing power that is about to be unleashed on the golf ball.

STEP 5

All of rotation, torquing, releasing, driving, transferring, sequencing, and extending come together at one moment, just after impact. If the building blocks leading up to impact are correct, you should breeze right through the ball to the point of fully expended energy. Hitting little shots and stopping this point of culmination is one of the best things you can do for your swing. It allows you to pitch the ball, deliver the club with some forward shaft lean, and control the trajectory of the shot.

Step 6

What some people see in the perfect dismount of an Olympic gymnast, or the landing of a figure skater after a triple axel, I see in a proper follow-through: effortless, balanced, and poised. I suggest holding your finish for just a moment. It allows you to recall the feeling of the swing, not to mention improve your balance and consistency.

www.ingramcontent.com/pod-product-compliance
Lightning Source LLC
Chambersburg PA
CBHW080442170426
43195CB00017B/2864